GW0985372

Legorreta + Legorreta

Legorreta + Legorreta

teNeues

Editor in chief:
Paco Asensio

Editor and original texts:
Aurora Cuito

Photographs:
Lourdes Legorreta

English translation:
William Bain

German translation:
Bettina Beck

French translation:
Michel Ficerai

Italian translation:
Giovanna Carnevali

Art direction:
Mireia Casanovas Soley

Graphic design / Layout:
Emma Termes Parera and Soti Mas-Bagà

Published worldwide by teNeues Publishing Group
(except Spain, Portugal and South-America):

teNeues Verlag GmbH + Co. KG
Am Selder 37, 47906 Kempen, Germany
Tel.: 0049-(0)2152-916-0
Fax: 0049-(0)2152-916-111

teNeues Publishing Company
16 West 22nd Street, New York, N.Y., 10010, USA
Tel.: 001-212-627-9090
Fax: 001-212-627-9511

teNeues Publishing UK Ltd.
Aldwych House, 71/91 Aldwych
London WC2B 4HN, UK
Tel.: 0044-1892-837-171
Fax: 0044-1892-837-272

www.teneues.com

Editorial project:

© 2002 **LOFT** Publications
Domènech 9, 2-2
08012 Barcelona. Spain
Tel.: 0034 93 218 30 99
Fax: 0034 93 237 00 60
e-mail: loft@loftpublications.com
www.loftpublications.com

Printed by:
Gráficas Anman.
Barcelona, Spain

May 2002

Die Deutsche Bibliothek – CIP-Einheitsaufnahme
Ein Titeldatensatz für diese Publikation ist bei der Deutschen Bibliothek erhältlich.

ISBN: 3-8238-5589-1

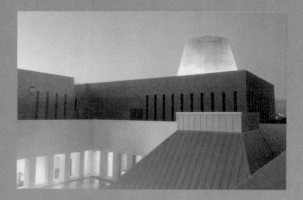

In spite of its monumentality, the architecture of Legorreta + Legorreta is conceived for us to live in: it suits our needs, our appetites, and our emotions. The buildings not only guarantee the functionalism and the comfort of the use of space, they also evoke autochthonous cultural tradition and stimulate the senses.

Legorreta + Legorreta create a special architectural universe thanks to an intense relationship with the clients, an attentive view of the settings, successful building strategies, and an ingenious poetic sensitivity.

Vernacular techniques serve the architects as inspiration to do homage to the past, to create an interface with the memory of construction, to regain traditional spaces, such as the square, the temple, or the patio. These plain spaces favor communication and social harmony. A good example of this savoir faire may be seen in the vestibules of the Center of Visual arts and of the Sheraton Hotel in Bilbao. Geometry allows them to generate pure and timeless forms that instill rotundity and clarity into the complicated projects. The structural design and the functions intermingle, creating simple distributions that make the inhabitants' movements easy. Even in large complexes, like the Chiron Laboratories, or the EGADE Graduate School, privacy and simplicity is preserved, two characteristics of the Latin American architecture which Legorreta + Legorreta have empowered.

The treatment of light aids them in creating different spaces without any need of raising walls or separators. They combine shadows, the capricious reflections in water, and the iridescence of different finishings to bring off optimal arrangements for work, relaxation, or dreaming.

The application of color strikes Legorreta + Legorreta as being of the first priority, above all in the projects set in their native Mexico. It is a country where color makes up a part of daily life, from the browns and greens of the mountains to the intense reds in the food and the traditional clothing. They are, all of them, tones that the architects use to dramatize spaces, to intensify the personal experience of the people in the buildings.

With all of these ingredients, Legorreta + Legorreta integrate architecture, landscaping, and interior decoration into a single discipline that respects the place, the traditions, and the people it makes contact with.

Die Architektur von Legorreta + Legorreta ist trotz ihrer wahrhaftigen Monumentalität für den Menschen gedacht und gemäß seinen Bedürfnissen, Vorlieben und Gefühlen gestaltet. Bei den Objekten sind nicht nur Funktionalität und Komfort der Räume gewährleistet, sondern sie lehnen sich zudem an die örtliche kulturelle Tradition an und stimulieren die Sinne. Legorreta + Legorreta schaffen ihr ganz eigenes architektonisches Universum dank der intensiven Beziehungen mit den Kunden, eines stets aufmerksamen Blickes auf die Umgebung, gelungener baulicher Strategien sowie einer geistreichen Empfindsamkeit für Poesie.

Sie bedienen sich einheimischer Techniken als Inspiration für eine Huldigung an die Vergangenheit, um einen Zugang zum architektonischen Erbe zu schaffen und auch um die ursprüngliche Rolle von traditionellen Orten, wie dem Marktplatz, der Kirche oder dem Hof wieder aufleben zu lassen. Diese gemeinschaftlichen Räume begünstigen die Kommunikation und das harmonische Zusammenleben der Menschen. Ein gutes Beispiel für dieses savoir faire sind die Eingangshallen des Zentrums für visuelle Kunst und des Sheraton-Hotels in Bilbao. Mit Hilfe der Geometrie erzeugen sie reine und zeitlose Formen, die den komplizierten Projekten ihre runde Klarheit verleihen. Formlinien und Funktionen vermischen sich und schaffen einfache Strukturen, die die Mobilität der Nutzer unterstützen. Sogar bei großen Objekten wie den Chiron-Laboratorien oder der Graduiertenschule EGADE, werden die Privatsphäre und die Einfachheit aufrecht erhalten. Dies sind Merkmale der lateinamerikanischen Architektur, die Legorreta + Legorreta zu betonen wissen.

Sie erschaffen ganz verschiedenartige Räume durch den Umgang mit Licht, der Wände oder Raumteilungen unnötig macht. Sie kombinieren Schatten, die eigenwilligen Reflexe des Wassers und das Schillern in allen Regenbogenfarben einiger Oberflächenfinishs und erfinden so optimale Räume zum Arbeiten, Entspannen oder Träumen.

Der Farbauftrag ist für sie vor allem bei den Projekten für ihr Geburtsland Mexiko vorrangig, wo die Farbe Teil des täglichen Lebens ist, von den Braun- und Grüntönen der Berge bis hin zum intensiven Rot der Speisen und der traditionellen Kleidung. Diese gesamte Farblichkeit setzen sie ein, um die Raumdramatik und mit ihr das persönliche Erleben der Nutzer zu steigern.

Mit diesen Zutaten lassen Legorreta + Legorreta Architektur, Landschaftsgestaltung und Innenarchitektur zu einer einzigen Disziplin verschmelzen, die von großem Respekt vor der Umgebung, den Traditionen und den Menschen geprägt ist.

L'architecture de Legorreta + Legorreta, bien que monumentale, est pensée pour l'homme, adaptée à ses besoins, à ses attentes et à ses émotions. Les oeuvres assurent non seulement la fonctionnalité et le confort des espaces mais évoquent également la tradition culturelle autochtone et stimulent les sens. Legorreta + Legorreta créent un univers architectural particulier grâce à une relation intense avec les clients, à un regard attentif sur l'environnement, à des stratégies de construction avisées et à une sensibilité poétique ingénieuse.

Les techniques vernaculaires sont leur source d'inspiration afin de rendre hommage au passé, créer un lien avec la mémoire constructive ou récupérer les lieux traditionnels, comme la place, le temple ou le patio. Ces espaces communs favorisent la communication et l'harmonie de la cohabitation. Les halls d'entrée du Centre des arts visuels et de l'hôtel Sheraton de Bilbao constituent de bons exemples de ce savoir-faire. La géométrie leur permet de générer des formes pures et intemporelles qui offrent éclat et clarté aux projets complexes. Parcours et fonctions se marient pour créer des distributions simples qui facilitent la mobilité des usagers. Même dans les complexes importants, comme les Laboratoires Chirón ou l'école de commerce EGADE, sont préservés l'intimité et la simplicité, deux caractéristiques de l'architecture latino-américaine que Legorreta + Legorreta ont su valoriser.

Le traitement de la lumière les aide à créer des espaces divers sans devoir monter ni murs ni séparations. Combinant les ombres, les reflets capricieux

de l'eau et l'iridescence de certaines finitions pour inventer des environnements parfaits où travailler, se reposer ou rêver.

Le rôle des couleurs leur paraît primordial, surtout pour les projets situés au Mexique, un pays où elles sont parties prenantes de la vie quotidienne, des marrons ou des verts des montagnes jusqu'aux rouges intenses de la nourriture et des costumes traditionnels. Des tonalités toutes mises à contribution pour théâtraliser les espaces et intensifier l'expérience personnelle des usagers.

À l'aide de tous ces ingrédients, Legorreta + Legorreta intègrent architecture, paysagisme et design d'intérieur en une seule discipline respectueuse de son environnement, des traditions et des personnes.

Nonostante il carattere di monumentalità che la contraddistingue, l'architettura di Legorreta + Legorreta é stata pensata a "misura d'uomo", per rispondere alle sue esigenze, alle sue emozioni e per soddisfare i suoi desideri. I lavori di questo architetto non garantiscono soltanto la funzionalità ed il confort degli spazi, ma rievocano anche la tradizione culturale autoctona stuzzicando i gusti.

L'architettura di Legorreta + Legorreta , molto sensibile all'intorno costruito e alla cultura locale, crea attorno a sé un peculiare universo architettonico grazie anche a una intensa relazione con i clienti e a determinate strategiche scelte costruttive.

Si ispira alle tecniche vernacolari per rendere omaggio al passato, per marcare un vincolo con la memoria del costruito, per recuperare particolari spazi legati alla tradizione, come per esempio la piazza, il tempio o il patio. Questi luoghi sociali favoriscono la comunicazione e un' armoniosa convivenza. Un buon esempio di questo savoir faire sono gli ingressi del Centro di Arti Visuali dell'hotel Sheraton a Bilbao. La geometria gli permette di generare forme pure e "senza tempo" che conferiscono rotondità e chiarezza ai progetti complessi. I percorsi e le funzioni si mescolano tra loro creando distribuzioni semplici che facilitano il flusso degli utenti. L'attenzione alla privacy e alla semplicità, proprie dell'architettura latino-americana di Legorreta + Legorreta, si può avvertire anche nei grandi complessi come per esempio nei Laboratori Chiron o nella Scuola di Specializzazione. Attraverso il trattamento della luce riescono a creare spazi differenti secondo le necessità senza ricorrere alla costruzioni di pareti o tramezze. Giocano con le ombre, con i riflessi cangianti dell'acqua, con con la riflessione di alcuni materiali per interni al fine di inventare nuovi ambienti e ottimizzare quelli lavorativi o quelli dedicati al relax. L'applicazione del colore risulta materica soprattutto nei progetti realizzati nel Messico natale, paese dove il colore é parte integrante della vita quotidiana; dalle tonalità marroni come quelle della terra ai verdi delle montagne e persino agli intensi rossi dei cibi e dei vestiti tradizionali. Sono tutte tonalità utilizzate per drammatizzare gli spazi, per intensificare le sensazioni personali di ciascuna persona.

Con tutti questi ingredienti, Legorreta + Legorreta integrano architettura, paesaggismo ed interiorismo racchiudendoli in un'unica disciplina che nutre rispetto per l'intorno, per le tradizioni e per le persone.

Office Building

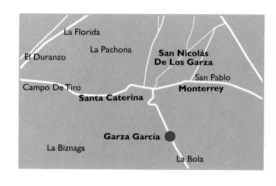

Av. Real San Agustín, 304
Monterrey, Mexico
1995

The sculptural form of this office building in Monterrey was given by the triangular shape of the site and by its industrial environment. The two pieces are comprised of different bodies, patios, and terraces that look out onto the mountains and the city. One of the buildings was destined to house the offices of the director of the Museum of Modern Art of Monterrey, a passionate collector. The ground floor has a reception area and an exhibition space; the first floor is for the offices; and the second contains the main office, a conference room, a library, and a kitchen with dining room and living room. Every corner, needless to say, includes artwork. The other building also has three stories and contains offices for rent.

Die Form dieses Bürogebäudes in Monterrey mutet aufgrund der dreieckigen Geometrie des Geländes und der industriellen Umgebung wie eine Skulptur an. Die beiden Blöcke setzen sich aus verschiedenen Volumen, Höfen und Terrassen mit Blick auf die Berge und die Stadt zusammen. In einem der Gebäude sind die Büroräume des Direktors des Museums für zeitgenössische Kunst von Monterrey, eines leidenschaftlichen Kunstsammlers, untergebracht. Das Erdgeschoss umfasst einen Empfangs- und einen Ausstellungsraum, das erste Obergeschoss die Büros. Im zweiten Obergeschoss befinden sich das Hauptbüro, ein Konferenzraum, eine Bibliothek, sowie eine Küche mit Ess- und Wohnzimmer. Es erübrigt sich zu sagen, dass sich in jedem Winkel ein Kunstwerk befindet. Das andere Gebäude besteht ebenfalls aus drei Ebenen und beherbergt Mietbüros.

La forme sculpturale de cet immeuble de bureaux de la ville de Monterrey naît de la géométrie triangulaire du terrain et de son environnement industriel. Les deux bâtiments souhaités sont composés de différents volumes, patios et terrasses avec des vues sur les montagnes et la ville. L'un des édifices a pour objet d'accueillir les bureaux du directeur du Musée d'art contemporain de Monterrey, un collectionneur passionné. Le rez-de-chaussée abrite une réception et une salle d'exposition, le premier étage les bureaux et le second le bureau principal, une salle de réunion, une bibliothèque et une cuisine dotée d'une salle à manger et d'un salon. Point n'est besoin de préciser que chaque recoin est rehaussé d'une œuvre d'art. L'autre construction, également sur trois niveaux, héberge des bureaux en location.

La forma scultorea di questo edificio per uffici a Monterrey derivò dalla forma triangolare del lotto e dal contesto industriale in cui si ubica l'intervento. I due edifici richiesti sono costituiti da differenti volumi, cortili e terrazze con viste verso le montagne e la città. Si decise che uno dei due edifici ospitasse gli uffici del direttore del Museo di Arte Contemporanea di Monterrey, un appassionato collezionista. Il pianterreno accoglie la reception ed una sala per esposizioni, mentre il primo piano gli spazi degli uffici; nel secondo piano incontriamo invece l'ufficio principale, una sala per riunioni, una biblioteca ed una cucina con soggiorno e sala da pranzo. È superfluo notare quanto ogni angolo sia stato curato come una vera e propria opera d'arte. Anche l'altra costruzione consta di tre livelli e contiene uffici per affitto.

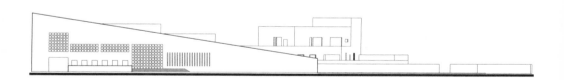

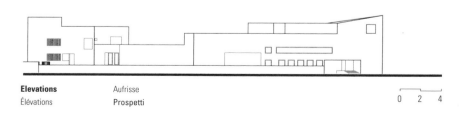

Elevations   Aufrisse

Élévations   Prospetti

0   2   4

Technological Museum of Innovation

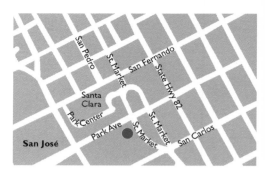

201 S. Market Street
San José, California, U.S.A.
1998

The museum, in the heart of San José, not only enriches the urban environment it consolidates, but also successfully resolves the functional program the clients proposed. Conceived as a large horizontal block, the building opens according to the needs of the interior. Hence, the entranceways were provided with windows, as were the façades adjacent to the patios, the exhibition rooms, and the projection room, which is fitted with a large hemispherical screen. The facings inside this room are in an exuberant ceramic texture; outside, glazed tiles cover a magnificent roof. The museum rises up like the large cultural and educational center it is: the perception of the space is also a new experience.

Das im Herzen von San José gelegene Museum ist nicht nur eine Bereicherung für die festgefügte urbane Umgebung, sondern meistert auch erfolgreich das von den Kunden vorgeschlagene funktionelle Konzept. Das Gebäude wurde als großer horizontaler Block angelegt, der sich gemäß der Bedürfnisse des Inneren öffnet. Die Fassaden wurden für Eingänge, Höfe sowie Fenster des Geschäfts und des Restaurants durchbrochen. Die Haupteingangshalle empfängt die Besucher und verbindet zwei große Höfe, die Ausstellungsräume und den Vorführungsraum, der über eine große, halbkugelförmige Leinwand verfügt. Das Innere dieses Saals ist großzügig mit Keramik ausgestattet und außen mit Glaskacheln verkleidet, so dass als Erkennungsmerkmal des Gebäudes ein Aufsehen erregendes Dach entstand. Das Museum versteht sich als großes Kulturzentrum, bei dem die Wahrnehmung des Raumes ganz neue Erfahrungsbereiche eröffnet.

Le musée, situé au cœur de San José, a non seulement enrichi un environnement urbain consolidé mais également résolu avec succès le programme fonctionnel que les clients avaient proposé. Le bâtiment a été conçu comme un grand bloc horizontal qui s'ouvre, selon les impératifs intérieurs ; des ouvertures ont été percées pour les entrées dans la façade et pour les patios et les baies vitrées de la boutique et du restaurant. Le hall principal accueille les visiteurs et connecte deux vastes patios, les salles d'exposition et la salle de projection, dotée d'un grand écran hémisphérique. L'intérieur de cette salle est revêtu d'une texture céramique exubérante et son extérieur de mosaïques en verre, créant une couverte spectaculaire conférant son identité à la construction. Le musée se dresse comme un grand centre culturel et éducatif, au sein duquel la perception de l'espace constitue aussi une nouvelle expérience.

Il Museo, ubicato nel centro di Santa Josè, non solo ha arricchito il contesto urbano già consolidato, ma ha anche risolto con successo il programma funzionale che veniva richiesto dalla committenza. L'edificio è stato concepito come un blocco orizzontale che si apre a seconda delle necessità provenienti dall'interno, con le facciate ritagliate in corrispondenza delle entrate, dei cortili e delle grandi finestre del negozio e del ristorante. L'atrio principale accoglie i visitatori e collega due grandi cortili, la sala espositiva e la sala per le proiezioni, dotata di un grande schermo emisferico. All'interno, questa sala è stata trattata con un'esuberante rivestimento ceramico, mentre la pelle esterna è costituita da piastrelle di vetro che definiscono una cupola molto vistosa caratteristica dell'edificio. Il Museo si erge come un grande centro culturale ed educativo dove anche la percezione dello spazio pretende essere un'esperienza nuova.

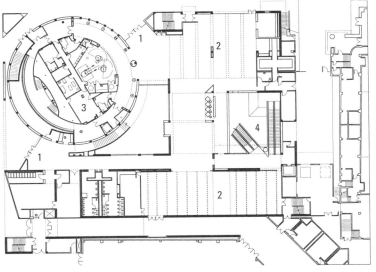

1. **Access**	1. Eingang
2. **Exhibition rooms**	2. Ausstellungsräum
3. **Offices**	3. Büroräume
4. **Access to the superior floors**	4. Zugang zu den oberen Ebenen
1. Accès	1. Accessi
2. Sales d'exposition	2. Sale espositive
3. Bureaux	3. Amministrazione
4. Accès aux étages supérieures	4. Accesso ai pian superiori

Ground floor   Erdgeschoss

Rez-de-chaussée   Piano Terra

0   5   10

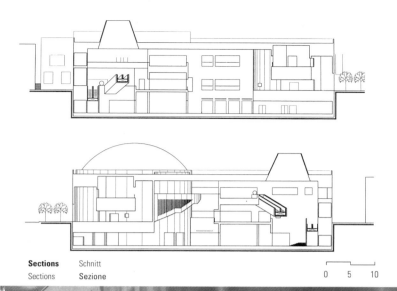

Sections   Schnitt
Sections   **Sezione**

0   5   10

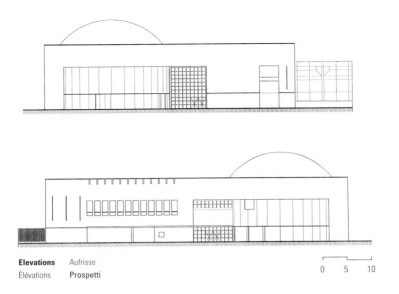

Elevations   Aufrisse
Élévations   **Prospetti**

0   5   10

Los Patios Residential Complex

Mexico City, Mexico
1998

In the Mexican capital, the lack of habitable space has increased considerably in the last few years. This problem not only concerns the lower classes, since today's young people, once accustomed to living in enormous houses, now have to be satisfied with homes of reduced dimensions. Los Patios offers dwellings which, in spite of being small, enjoy ample surroundings where the luxury lies in the space itself and not in the materials or the finishings. The intense relationship between the architects, the promoter, and some of the clients was enough to satisfy the questions of cost for some and the functional requirements for others. Each apartment has a gardened patio with a fountain and high walls toward which the rooms of the house spill out. The wall height itself, the oversize windows, and the colors emphasize the brightness of the interiors.

La capitale mexicaine fait face ces dernières années à une véritable pénurie de surface habitable. Ce problème ne concerne pas uniquement les classes défavorisées. En effet, les jeunes auparavant habitués à vivre dans de vastes demeures doivent se contenter aujourd'hui de foyers aux dimensions réduites. Los Patios propose des logements qui, en dépit d'une superficie comptée, jouissent d'atmosphères spacieuses où l'espace lui-même constitue le luxe et non les matériaux ou les finitions. L'intense relation entre les architectes, le promoteur et certains de ses clients a permis de satisfaire les impératifs économiques des uns et les besoins fonctionnels des autres. Chaque logement dispose d'un patio paysager doté d'une fontaine et de murs élevés que surplombent les pièces de la maison. L'élévation des toits, les grandes fenêtres et le travail chromatique sur les parois soulignent encore la luminosité des intérieurs.

In der mexikanischen Hauptstadt ist der Mangel an Wohnfläche in den letzten Jahren beträchtlich gewachsen. Dieses Problem betrifft nicht nur die unteren Gesellschaftsschichten, da sich nun auch die heutigen jungen Menschen, die daran gewöhnt waren, in riesigen Wohnungen zu leben, mit kleineren Wohnungen zufriedengeben müssen. Los Patios besteht aus Wohnräumen, die trotz geringer Flächen weitläufige Zimmer bieten, wo der Luxus nicht in den verwendeten Materialien oder den Oberflächenfinishs, sondern im Raum an sich besteht. Die enge Beziehung zwischen den Architekten, den Bauherren und einigen der Kunden diente dazu, sowohl die finanziellen Bedürfnisse der einen als auch die funktionellen Ansprüche der anderen zu befriedigen. Jede Wohnung besitzt einen Hof mit Garten, einen Brunnen und hohe Mauern, zu dem hin die Zimmer des Hauses gerichtet sind. Die Höhe der Decken, die großen Fenster und die farbliche Gestaltung der Wände heben die Helligkeit der Innenräume hervor.

Nella capitale messicana, la mancanza di suolo urbanizzabile si è considerevolmente aggravata in questi ultimi anni. Il problema interessa non solo le classi modeste, dal momento che ormai anche i giovani, un tempo abituati a vivere in case enormi, oggi devono abituarsi ad appartamenti di dimensioni ridotte. Los Patios offre abitazioni che, nonostante una superficie ridotta, godono di ambienti ampi, dove il lusso risiede nello Spazio propriamente detto piuttosto che nelle finiture o nei dettagli. La stretta relazione tra i progettisti, il promotore ed alcuni dei clienti rese possibile la conciliazione delle esigenze economiche degli uni con le richieste funzionali degli altri. Ogni appartamento possiede un cortile con fontana e giardino ed alti muri da cui si affacciano le camere della casa. L'altezza dei soffitti, le grandi finestre ed il trattamento cromatico delle pareti enfatizza la luminosità degli interni.

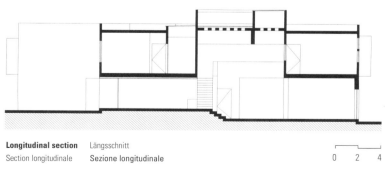

Longitudinal section   Längsschnitt

Section longitudinale   **Sezione longitudinale**

0   2   4

Ground floor   Erdgeschoss
Rez-de-chaussée   Piano Terra

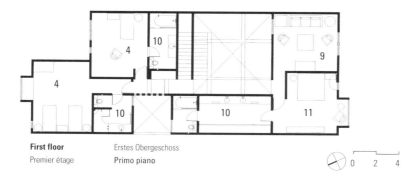

First floor   Erstes Obergeschoss
Premier étage   Primo piano

1. Access	1. Eingang
2. Garage	2. Garage
3. Bath	3. Badezimmer
4. Bedrooms	4. Schlafzimmer
5. Laundry	5. Waschküche
6. Court	6. Innenhof
7. Kitchen	7. Küche
8. Dining room	8. Esszimmer
9. Living room	9. Wohnzimmer
10. Bathrooms	10. Badezimmer
11. Master bedroom	11. Schlafzimmer

1. Accès	1. Ingresso
2. Garage	2. Garage
3. Salle de bains	3. Bagno
4. Chambres	4. Camera da letto
5. Buanderie	5. Zona di servizio
6. Terrasse	6. Cortile
7. Cuisine	7. Cucina
8. Salle à manger	8. Sala da parnzo
9. Salle de séjour	9. Salotto
10. Salles de bains	10. Bagnos
11. Chambre principale	11. Camere da letto

0   2   4

Corporate Television Center

Vasco de Quiroga, 2000
Colonia Santa Fe, Mexico
1998

The Corporate Television Center is part of an urbanistic development by Legorreta + Legorreta that is called Santa Fé. It includes office buildings, a large mall, exclusive residential areas, and educational centers. Access to the impressive Santa Fé building is through a square, both for pedestrians and vehicles. The offices are distributed through five buildings connected by porticos with arched ceilings. Each of these joins the vestibules with stairways, elevators, and service zones. The buildings have a personality all their own so that the project may be read as a complex or as a grouping of different owners. This in itself confers on the center a good deal of flexibility. The hi-tech offices enjoy views of the many green zones surrounding the complex.

Das Centro Corporativo Televisa ist Teil eines städtebaulichen Entwicklungskonzepts von Legorreta + Legorreta mit dem Namen Santa Fé. Es umfasst Bürogebäude, ein großes Einkaufszentrum und pädagogische Einrichtungen. Der Zugang zu dem großartigen Sitz von Televisa erfolgt für Fahrzeuge und Fußgänger gleichermaßen über einen Platz. Die Büros sind über fünf Gebäude verteilt, die durch Portalgebäude mit bogenförmigen Dächern verbunden sind. Diese verbinden jeweils die Eingangshallen mit den Treppenhäusern, den Aufzügen und den Servicebereichen. Jedes der Gebäude hat seinen eigenen Stil, so dass das Projekt als ein Ganzes oder aber als eine Ansammlung von Gebäuden verschiedener Eigentümer betrachtet werden kann. Diese Eigenschaft verleiht dem Zentrum eine große Einsatzflexibilität. Die Büros sind mit modernster Technik ausgestattet und gewähren einen Blick auf die zahlreichen Grünbereiche der Anlage.

Le siège social de Televisa fait partie d'une œuvre de développement urbanistique de Legorreta + Legorreta baptisée Santa Fe. Elle comprend des immeubles de bureaux, un grand centre commercial, des zones résidentielles à accès restreint et des centres éducatifs. Une place propose l'accès au magnifique siège social de Televisa, tant pour les piétons que pour les véhicules. Les bureaux se répartissent entre cinq immeubles connectés par des portiques voûtés qui, chacun, unissent les halls d'entrée avec les escaliers, les ascenseurs et les zones de service. Chaque bâtiment est doté d'une personnalité en propre et le projet peut, de ce fait, être lu comme un ensemble ou comme un regroupement de différents propriétaires, conférant au centre une ample flexibilité d'usage. Les bureaux disposent d'un technologie de pointe et jouissent de points de vue sur les nombreux espaces verts du complexe.

La sede della società Televisa fa parte parte di un progetto di scala urbanistica sviluppato da Legorreta+Legorreta chiamato Santa Fè ed include edifici per uffici, un grande centro commerciale, aree residenziali di alto standing e centri educativi. L'accesso che conduce alla fiammante sede di Televisa avviene, tanto per i pedoni quanto per i veicoli, attraverso una piazza. Gli uffici sono distribuiti in cinque edifici collegati tra di loro mediante portici voltati che, per ciascuno di essi, uniscono gli atrii con i corpi scala, gli ascensori e le zone di servizio. Ogni edificio possiede un suo proprio carattere, dimodochè il progetto può leggersi con carattere unitario, oppure come una aggregazione di differenti proprietari, caratteristica questa che conferisce al centro una notevole flessibilità d'uso. Gli uffici sono dotati di tecnologie d'avanguardia e godono di vista verso le numerose aree verdi del complesso.

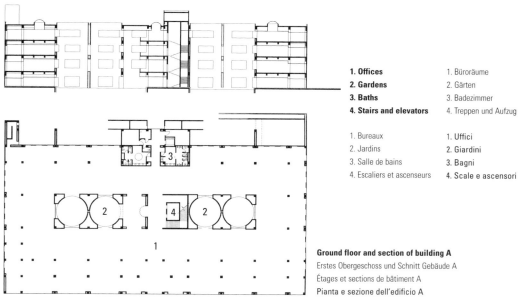

1. Offices   1. Büroräume

2. Gardens   2. Gärten

3. Baths   3. Badezimmer

4. Stairs and elevators   4. Treppen und Aufzug

1. Bureaux   1. Uffici

2. Jardins   2. Giardini

3. Salle de bains   3. Bagni

4. Escaliers et ascenseurs   **4. Scale e ascensori**

Ground floor and section of building A
Erstes Obergeschoss und Schnitt Gebäude A
Étages et sections de bâtiment A
Pianta e sezione dell'edificio A

0   5   10

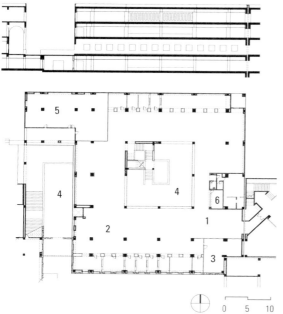

1. Reception   1. Empfang
2. Offices   2. Büroräume
3. Archives   3. Archive
4. Gardens   4. Gärten
5. Gymnasium   5. Fitness-Raum
6. Meeting room   6. Konferenzzimmer

1. Reception   1. Reception
2. Bureaux   2. Uffici
3. Archives   3. Archivi
4. Jardin   4. Giardino
5. Gymnase   5. Palestra
6. Salle de réunion   6. Sala per riunion

Ground floor and section of building B
Erstes Obergeschoss und Schnitt Gebäude B
Étages et sections de bâtiment B
Pianta e sezione dell'edificio B

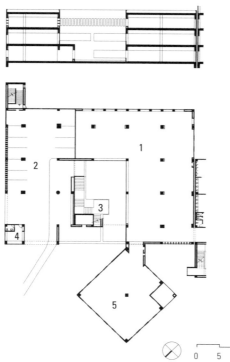

1. Offices	1. Büroräume
2. Parking	2. Parkplatz
3. Stairs and Elevation	3. Treppen und Aufzug
4. Warranty	4. Gebäudeschutz
5. Management	5. Management
1. Bureaux	1. Uffici
2. Parking	2. Parcheggio
3. Escaliers et ascenseurs	3. Scale e ascensori
4. Securité	4. Sicurezza
5. Direction	5. Direzione

Ground and section of building C
Erstes Obergeschoss und Schnitt Gebäude C
Étages et sections de bâtiment C
Pianta e sezione dell'edificio C

0 5 10

Visual Arts Center

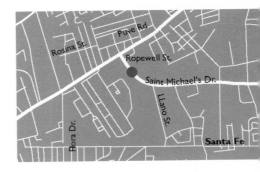

1.600 Saint Michael's Drive Santa Fe,
New Mexico, U.S.A.
1999

Santa Fe, in the course of the last few years, has seen the number of museums and art galleries grow notably. The city is fast becoming one of the most interesting cultural centers in the United States. The College of Santa Fe wanted to promote the educational aspects of such activities and thus commissioned Legorreta + Legorreta with a campus project to be developed over five years in two phases. The first phase consists in raising the College of Santa Fe Art Institute, the Visual Arts Center, the Marion Center for Photographic Arts, and the Art History Center. The second phase is a building with workshops and studios. The clients' objective is to create a complex that stimulates student creativity, makes it easy for the students to interact, and generates cultural activities at the College.

In den letzten Jahren ist die Zahl der Museen und Kunstgalerien in Santa Fe deutlich gestiegen, wodurch die Stadt zu einer der interessantesten Kulturzentren der Vereinigten Staate geworden ist. Die Universität von Santa Fe wollte die erzieherischen Aspekte solcher Aktivitäten verstärken und beauftragt Legorreta + Legorreta mit dem Bau eines Campus, dessen Aus führung sich in zwei Phasen über fünf Jahre erstrecken sollte Die erste Phase besteht im Bau des Santa Fe Art Institute, de Zentrums für visuelle Kunst, des Zentrums für Photokunst un des Zentrums für Kunstgeschichte. Die zweite Phase besteht ir Bau eines Werkstättengebäudes. Die Zielsetzung der Kunde und der Architekten ist die Erschaffung eines Komplexes, d die Kreativität der Schüler anregen, den Austausch zwische ihnen erleichtern soll und ebenso die kulturellen Aktivitäten de Universität fördert.

Ces dernières années, la ville de Santa Fe a vu croître ostensiblement le nombre de ses musées et galeries d'art et s'est ainsi convertie en l'un des centres culturels les plus intéressant des Etats-Unis. L'Université de Santa Fe souhaitait mettre l'accent sur les aspects éducatifs de ces activités et décida de charger Legorreta + Legorreta de construire un campus, développé en deux phases réparties sur cinq ans. La première consistait en l'édification de l'Institut artistique de Santa Fe, du Centre des arts visuels, du Centre des arts photographiques et du Centre d'histoire de l'art. La seconde étape était vouée à la construction d'un corps d'ateliers. Les clients et architectes avaient pour objectif commun la création d'un ensemble stimulant la créativité des élèves, facilitant leurs interactions et suscitant l'activité culturelle de l'Université.

Negli ultimi anni, la città di Santa Fe ha visto crescer considerevolmente il numero dei musei e delle galleri d'arte, situazione questa che ha fatto sì che la città s convertisse in uno dei centri culturali più interessar degli Stati Uniti. L'Università di Santa Fe voleva potenzi re gli aspetti educativi di queste attività e per quest motivo ha commissionato un campus che si realizzer nell'arco di cinque anni ed in due fasi. La prima fase co siste nell'erigere il Santa Fe Art Institute, il Centro di A Visive, il Centro di Arti Fotografiche ed il Centro di Stor dell'Arte. La seconda tappa consiste invece nella reali zazione di un edificio con laboratori. L'obiettivo di proge tisti e committenza è quello di generare un compless che stimoli la creatività degli allievi, che facili l'interazi ne fra di essi e che incoraggi le attività culturali dell'Un versità.

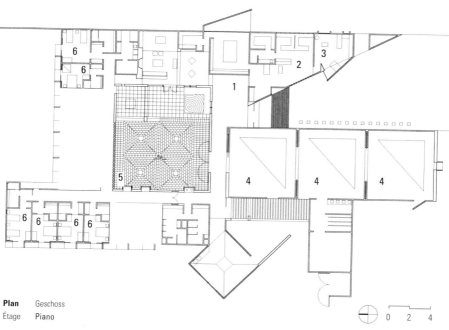

1. Access
2. Reception
3. Offices
4. Studies
5. Yard
6. Bedrooms

1. Eingang
2. Empfang
3. Büroräume
4. Arbeitszimmer
5. Innenhof
6. Schlafzimmer

1. Accès
2. Reception
3. Bureaux
4. Atelier
5. Terrasse
6. Chambres

1. Entrata
2. Reception
3. Ufficio
4. Studio
5. Cortile
6. Camere da letto

Plan   Geschoss
Étage   Piano

0   2   4

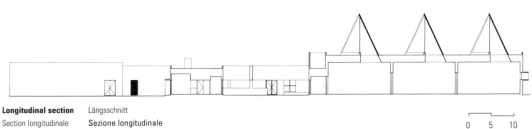

Longitudinal section   Längsschnitt

Section longitudinale   **Sezione longitudinale**

0   5   10

Elevation Aufriss
Élévation **Prospetto**

0   5   10

Chiron Laboratories

4560 Horton Street
Emeryville City, California, U.S.A.
1999

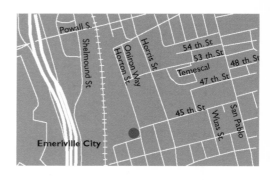

The Chiron Company commissioned Legorreta + Legorreta with the design of the urbanistic project for a large terrain on the eastern side of San Francisco Bay. The architects also took on the work of planning the new research center for Chiron. The latter's main aim was to put into practice its working philosophy in the guise of a singular building that improved its personnel communication. The architects went to work to achieve a functional project that would include privacy and security. It would also offer relaxed natural settings and a warm atmosphere. They decided to create a network of modules linked by patios and open spaces. Access to the complex would be effected by a large public square with an auditorium and a cafeteria; the laboratories would be ranged around covered patios with views of the Bay and the surrounding mountains.

Das Unternehmen Chiron gab Legorreta + Legorreta den Auftrag, den Bebauungsplan für ein großes Grundstück östlich der Bucht von San Francisco zu gestalten. Das Büro konzipierte gleichzeitig das neue Forschungszentrum des Unternehmens. Das Hauptziel des Kunden lag in der Wiedergabe seiner Arbeitsphilosopie in einem einzigartigen Gebäude, das die Kommunikation zwischen den Mitarbeitern begünstigen sollte. Die Herausforderung für die Architekten bestand darin, ein funktionelles Projekt zu erarbeiten, das Privatsphäre und Sicherheit gewährleisten und gleichzeitig entspannte Räume und eine warme Atmosphäre bieten sollte. Sie entschieden sich für ein Netzwerk aus durch Höfe und offene Räume miteinander verbundenen Modulen. Der Zugang zu dem Gebäudekomplex erfolgt über einen großen öffentlichen Platz mit einem Auditorium und einer Cafeteria. Die Labors hingegen gruppieren sich um überdachte Innenhöfe und gestatten den Blick auf die Bucht und die umliegenden Berge.

La société Chiron a confié à Legorreta + Legorreta tout à la fois la conception du plan urbanistique d'un grand terrain, situé à l'est de la baie de San Francisco, comme celle de son nouveau centre de recherche. Le client avait pour objectif principal la matérialisation de sa philosophie d'entreprise en un édifice singulier, susceptible de favoriser la communication de son personnel. Le défi pour les architectes consistait à créer un projet fonctionnel préservant intimité et sécurité tout en offrant des environnements sereins et une atmosphère chaleureuse. Le parti fut pris de créer un réseau de modules reliés par des patios et des espaces ouverts les entremêlant. Une grande place publique donne accès au complexe. Elle accueille un auditorium et une cafétéria alors que les laboratoires se distribuent autour de patios couverts disposant de vues sur la baie et les montagnes environnantes.

La compagnia Chiron incaricò la pianificazione urbanistica di un grande lotto ad est della baia di San Francisco e del nuovo Centro Ricerche della società. Il principale obiettivo del cliente era quello di ottenere la materializzazione della propria filosofia di lavoro in un singolo edificio in cui fosse favorita la comunicazione tra il proprio personale. Il compito dei progettisti era quello di ideare un progetto funzionale che godesse di privacy e sicurezza, ma che al tempo stesso offrisse ambienti rilassati ed una atmosfera accogliente. Si decise quindi di creare un sistema di moduli collegati per mezzo di cortili e spazi aperti che li relazionano vicendevolmente. L'accesso al compesso avviene attraverso una grande piazza pubblica dove si sono situati un auditorium ed una caffetteria, mentre i laboratori sono stati ordinati intorno ai cortili coperti con vista verso la baia e le montagne circostanti.

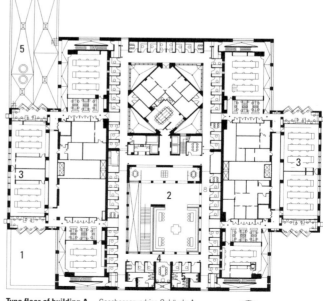

1. Yard	1. Innenhof
2. Waiting room	2. Warteraum
3. Offices	3. Büroräume
4. Meeting room	4. Konferenzzimmer
5. Roof	5. Dach
1. Terrasse	1. Cortili
2. Pièce d'attente	**2. Sale espositive**
3. Bureaux	**3. Uffici**
4. Salle de réunion	**4. Toilettes**
5. Toit	**5. Patio**

Type floor of building A   Geschossgrundriss Gebäude A

Type étage de bâtiment A   **Pianta Tipo dell'edificio A**

0   5   10

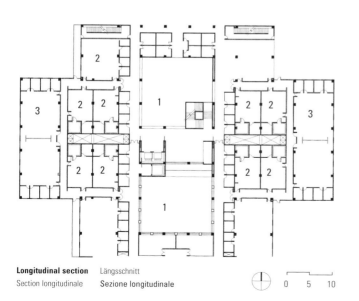

Longitudinal section   Längsschnitt
Section longitudinale   Sezione longitudinale

0   5   10

1. Yard	1. Innenhof
2. Office	2. Warteraum
3. Meeting room	3. Konferenzraum
1. Terrasse	1. Cortili
2. Bureaux	2. Uffici
3. Salle de réunion	3. Sale per riunioni

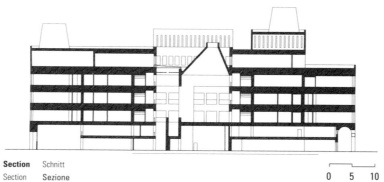

Section   Schnitt
Section   Sezione

0   5   10

Chiron Laboratories | **47**

Reno House

Reno, Nevada, U.S.A.
1999

The distinctive environment of rocks and low shrubs brought about a sculptural and abstract house that respects the landscape and also protects itself from the area's strong winds. High walls organize the site and provide the house and its patios with privacy. The simple geometrical shapes and limited number of materials make for a serene house almost evocative of the monastery. The natural illumination in the complex was guaranteed through a complete system of doors, windows, and skylights, bringing in different intensities of light. The owners wanted a high-profile role for their art collection, hence the rooms are clean and simple bays. The garden, where the only intentional touch is some local rocks, keeps to the spirit of the landscape with its autochthonous vegetation.

Die eigentümliche Umgebung aus Felsen und Sträuchern ließ ein Haus mit skulpturartigen und abstrakten Formen entstehen, das einerseits die Landschaft respektiert und andererseits vor den heftigen Winden in diesem Gebiet schützt. Das Grundstück ist von großen Mauern durchzogen, die dem Wohnhaus seine Privatsphäre geben. Die Struktur des Hauses wird durch einen großen Hof vorgegeben. Das gesamte Objekt ist von nahezu mönchischer Strenge gezeichnet: einfache geometrische Formen und der sparsame Umgang mit Materialien gestalten ein Haus, das die heitere Ruhe antiker Klöster ausstrahlt. Die Beleuchtung wird durch ein komplexes System aus Öffnungen, Fenstern und Oberlichtern gewährleistet, die das Licht mit unterschiedlicher Intensität ins Innere einfallen lassen. Die Eigentümer wollten ihrer Kunstsammlung eine vorrangige Stellung einräumen, weshalb die Räume des Hauses einfach und schmucklos sind und einen ungehinderten Kunstgenuss ermöglichen. Der Garten, in dem lediglich vereinzelt einige Felsen aus der Umgebung arrangiert wurden, erhält dank der örtlichen Vegetation den Geist der Landschaft aufrecht.

L'environnement particulier de roches et d'arbustes a formé une maison sculpturale et abstraite qui, tout en respectant le paysage, protège des vents violents qui balayent la région. De grands murs distribuent le terrain et préservent une certaine intimité, la maison s'organisant autour d'un vaste patio. Une austérité quasi-monacale régit tout le projet : peu de matériaux et des formes géométriques simples pour une maison sereine évoquant d'antiques monastères. L'éclairage de l'ensemble est assuré par un système complexe d'ouvertures, de fenêtres et de claires-voies qui laissent pénétrer différentes intensités de lumière. Les propriétaires souhaitant mettre en valeur leur collection artistique et les pièces sont ainsi constituées de volumes simples et clairs qui permettent de profiter des œuvres. Le jardin, où seuls quelques rochers de la région furent placés intentionnellement, perpétue l'esprit du paysage grâce à la végétation autochtone.

Il peculiare contesto di rocce ed arbusti bassi, fece sì che la casa si configurasse come scultorea ed astratta, rispettuosa del paesaggio nel suo proteggersi dai forti venti che soffiano nella zona. Alcuni grandi muri organizzano il lotto e conferiscono privacy alla villa, organizzata intorno ad un ampio cortile. Una austerità quasi monacale regola tutto il progetto: forme geometriche semplici e pochi materiali definiscono una casa tranquilla che evoca l'atmosfera degli antichi monasteri. L'illuminazione del complesso è garantita da un ricercato sistema di aperture, finestre e lucernai che introducono la luce all'interno con differenti intensità. I proprietari desideravano dare protagonismo alla loro collezione d'arte e per questa ragione le stanze della villa sono volumi semplici e puliti che permettono di apprezzare le varie opere. Il giardino, in cui solamente si disposero alcune poche rocce provenienti dalla zona, mantiene intatto lo spirito del paesaggio grazie alla vegetazione autoctona.

1. Garage	1. Garage
2. Access court	2. Eingang
3. Dining rooms	3. Esszimmer
4. Kitchen	4. Küche
5. Living rooms	5. Wohnzimmer
6. Bedrooms	6. Schlafzimmer
7. Private zone	7. Private Zimmer

1. Garage	1. Garage
2. Accès	2. Cortile d'entrata
3. Salle à manger	3. Sala da pranzo
4. Cuisine	4. Cucina
5. Salle de sèjour	5. Salotto
6. Chambres	6. Stanze
7. Zone privée	7. Zona privata dei proprietari

Ground floor   Erdgeschoss   **First floor**   Erstes Obergeschoss
Rez de chaussée   **Piano Terra**   Premier Étage   **Primo Piano**   0   5   10

Cross section

Section perpendiculaire   Sezione trasversale

Längsschnitt

0   5   10

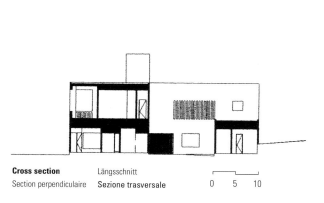

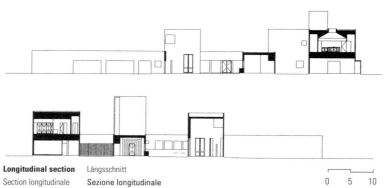

Longitudinal section Längsschnitt
Section longitudinale **Sezione longitudinale**

0 5 10

Córdova House

Mexico D.F., Mexico
2000

The Córdova House is in Lomas de Chapultepec, a neighborhood to the west of Mexico City, near a very affluent business zone. This inspired the architects to concentrate their energies on creating privacy for the houses. The building is set back some 16 feet from the street and nearly 10 feet from the other sides of the site because of a strict city ordinance. Hence, a transition area is also generated, giving a good deal of room between the public streets and the interiors of the houses. The domestic spaces are distributed on three stories: the subgrade level contains the service rooms, lighted naturally thanks to a patio. The ground floor houses the living areas on different levels, separated by short flights of stairs. On the first floor are the bedrooms, bathrooms, and dressing rooms. All of these rooms give onto patios, covered terraces, and gardened spaces that provide light and ventilation free of street noises.

Das Wohnhaus Córdova liegt in Lomas de Chapultepec, einem Stadtviertel im Westen von Mexiko-Stadt. In unmittelbarer Nähe befindet sich ein stark besuchtes Einkaufsviertel, weshalb die Architekten ihre Anstrengungen darauf konzentrierten, eine Privatsphäre für das Haus zu schaffen. Das Gebäude liegt fünf Meter hinter der Straßenlinie und drei Meter von den anderen Grenzen des Grundstücks entfernt, so wie es die strengen städtebaulichen Vorschriften der Stadt fordern. Auf diese Weise wurde auch ein Übergangsbereich als Puffer zwischen der öffentlichen Straße und dem Inneren des Hauses geschaffen. Die Räume sind auf drei Stockwerke verteilt: im Untergeschoss befinden sich die Serviceräume, die dank eines Hofes mit Tageslicht versorgt werden. Im Erdgeschoss befinden sich auf mehreren durch kleine Stufen getrennten Ebenen die Gemeinschaftsräume. Das erste Obergeschoss besteht aus Schlafzimmern, Bädern und Ankleideräumen. Sämtliche Räume des Hauses gehen auf Höfe, überdachte Terrassen und Gartenbereiche hinaus, die sie mit Licht und Luft versorgen und daher eine Öffnung zur lauten Straße hin unnötig machen.

La maison Córdova est située dans les Lomas de Chapultepec, un quartier à l'ouest du centre de México, proche d'une zone commerciale d'affluence. De ce fait, les architectes ont concentré leurs efforts sur la création d'intimité pour les logements. En raison des normes urbanistiques très strictes de cette zone, la maison est en retrait de cinq mètres en regard de la rue et de trois mètres des autres limites du terrain. Ainsi est générée une aire de transition, de respiration entre la voie publique et l'intérieur de la demeure. Les espaces domestiques se développent selon trois niveaux : le sous-sol abrite les dépendances du personnel, éclairées naturellement par un patio, le rez-de-chaussée accueille les salles communes sur des niveaux distincts séparés par quelques marches et le premier est dédié aux chambres, salles de bain et aux dressings. Toutes les pièces de la maison surplombent patios, terrasses couvertes et zones paysagères qui leur offrent lumière et aération sans nécessiter de s'ouvrir sur le tumulte de la rue.

Casa Córdova è situata in Lomas de Chapultepec, un quartiere ad ovest di Città del Messico vicino ad una zona commerciale con molo traffico, ragione questa che spinse i progettisti a concentrare i propri sforzi sulla ricerca della privacy. L'edificio, a causa della rigida normativa urbanistica, si ritrae di cinque metri rispetto alla strada e di tre rispetto agli altri limiti di lotto. In questo modo si genera uno spazio di transizione, di respiro, tra la via pubblica e l'interno della casa. Gli spazi domestici si sviluppano su tre livelli: il seminterrato accoglie i bagni di servizio illuminati naturalmente grazie ad un cortile, mentre il pianterreno ospita le stanze comuni che si articolano a distinte altezze, separate solo da alcuni pochi gradini; il primo piano infine comprende le stanze da letto, i bagni ed i guardaroba. Tutte le stanze della cas si affacciano su cortili, terrazze coperte e sono verdi che garantiscono luce e ventilazione senza che per questo ci si debba aprire al frastuono della strada.

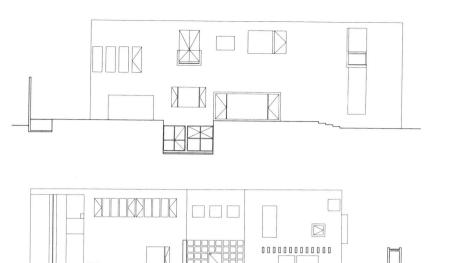

Elevations   Aufrisse
Élévations   Prospetti

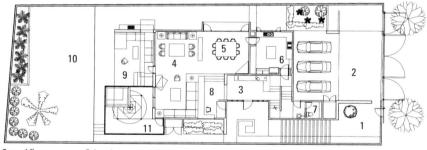

Ground floor   Erdgeschoss
Rez de chaussée   Piano Terra

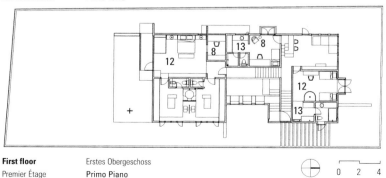

First floor   Erstes Obergeschoss
Premier Étage   Primo Piano

0   2   4

1. **Access**
2. **Garage**
3. **Hall**
4. **Living room**
5. **Dining room**
6. **Kitchen**
7. **Bath**
8. **Studies**
9. **Terrace**
10. **Garden**
11. **Fountain**
12. **Rooms**
13. **Baths**

1. Eingang
2. Garage
3. Diele
4. Wohnzimmer
5. Esszimmer
6. Küche
7. Badezimmer
8. Arbeitszimmer
9. Terrasse
10. Garten
11. Brunnen
12. Zimmer
13. Badezimmer

1. **Accès**
2. **Garage**
3. **Vestibule**
4. **Salle de séjour**
5. **Salle à manger**
6. **Cuisine**
7. **Salle de bains**
8. **Bureaux**
9. **Terrasse**
10. **Jardin**
11. **Fontaine**
12. **Chambres**
13. **Salle de bains**

1. Entrata
2. Garage
3. Vestibulo
4. Salotto
5. Sala da pranzo
6. Cucina
7. Bagno
8. Uffizi
9. Terrazza
9. Giardino
10. Fontana
11. Stanze
12. Stanza dei Giochi
13. Studio

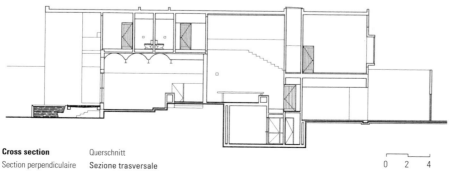

Cross section   Querschnitt

Section perpendiculaire   **Sezione trasversale**

0   2   4

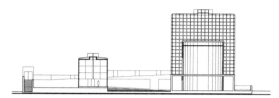

Mexico Pavilion, Expo Hannover 2000

Hannover, Germany
2000

0   5   10

The Mexico Pavilion is on a plain in the western part of the grounds of the Hannover International Fair. The project was carried out jointly with Enrique Krauze and the Museo del Niño "El Papalote", the result being like a museological screenplay divided into five themes, these being the five buildings linked by corridors that create new exhibition spaces. The gap in the buildings also creates different patios displaying the different ecosystems of Mexico: marine, desert, and jungle. As it is a temporary building, lightweight materials were used, such as glass and aluminum. These are easily set up and at the same time highly attractive. The color and texture blends with the particular way the light falls to recreate on an abstract level the country's character, culture, and spirit.

Der mexikanische Pavillon befindet sich auf einem ebenen Grundstück im Westen des Internationalen Messegeländes von Hannover. Das Projekt wurde zusammen mit Enrique Krauze und dem Museo del Niño (Kindermuseum) "El Papalote" bearbeitet. Das Ergebnis waren ein Programm und eine in fünf Themenbereiche untergliederte Museographie. Dieser entsprechen fünf in Form von Kreisläufen verbundene Gebäude, die neue Bereiche für Ausstellungen erschaffen. Durch die Trennung zwischen den Gebäuden entstehen zudem verschiedene Höfe, die abwechslungsreichen Ökosysteme Mexikos darstellen: Meer, Wüste und Urwald. Da es sich um ein auf Zeit angelegtes Gebäude handelt, wurden leichte Werkstoffe wie Glas und Aluminium verwendet, die einfach zu montieren sind und gleichzeitig eine sehr starke Wirkungskraft haben. Die Mischung aus Farben und Materialien spiegelt auf abstrakte Weise und zusammen mit der besonderen Lichtwirkung das Land, seinen Charakter, seine Kultur und seinen Geist wieder.

Le pavillon du Mexique est situé sur un terrain plat de la partie ouest du parc du Salon international de Hanovre. Le projet est le produit d'un travail en commun avec Enrique Krauze et le Musée de l'enfant de México (El Papalote) avec comme résultante un scénario et une muséographie s'articulant autour de cinq thèmes correspondant aux cinq bâtiments unis par des parcours créant de nouveaux espaces dans l'exposition. La séparation entre les constructions engendre, par surcroît, des patios distincts présentant les divers écosystèmes du Mexique : la mer, le désert et la jungle. La construction, s'inscrivant dans l'éphémère, a requis des matériaux légers, comme le cristal et l'aluminium, offrant à la fois un montage facile et jouissant d'une présence conséquente. Le mariage des couleurs et des textures ainsi que l'incidence particulière de la lumière matérialisent abstraitement le pays, sa personnalité, sa culture et son esprit.

Il padiglione del Messico era situato in un lotto piano nella parte ovest del recinto della Fiera Internazionale di Hannover. Il progetto fu realizzato insieme con Enrique Krauze ed il Museo del Bambino " El Papalote", dando come risultato una organizzazione ed una museografia strutturate secondo cinque temi, cui corrispondono cinque edifici uniti attraverso gli spazi di circolazione, in questo caso anch'essi utilizzati per esporre. La separazione tra i vari volumi crea inoltre differenti cortili in cui si presentano i vari ecosistemi del Messico: il mare, il deserto e la selva. Trattandosi di un edificio temporaneo, si utilizzarono materiali leggeri come il cristallo e l'alluminio, di facile montaggio ma al tempo stesso di efficace presenza.

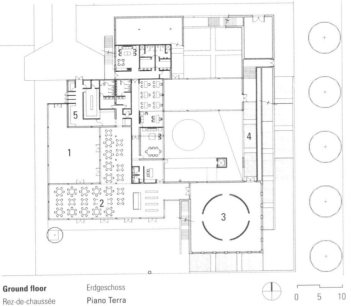

1. **Auditorium**	1. Auditorium
2. **Restaurant**	2. Restaurant
3. **Yart**	3. Innenhof
4. **Access to the superior floor**	4. Zugang zu den oberen Ebenen
5. **Kitchen**	5. Küche

1. Auditorium	1. **Auditorium**
2. Restaurant	2. **Ristorante**
3. Terrasse	3. **Cortile**
4. Accès aux étages supérieures	4. **Accesso ai piani superiori**
5. Cuisine	5. **Cucina**

| **Ground floor** | Erdgeschoss |
| Rez-de-chaussée | Piano Terra |

0   5   10

EGADE
Graduate School

Av. Fundadores & Av. Rufino Tamayo
Monterrey, Mexico
2001

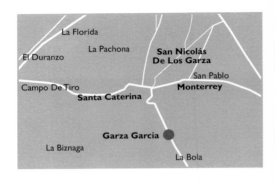

The aim of the Instituto Tecnológico de Estudios Superiores was to attract students and XOs to complete their studies in the Graduate School. Innovative programs were conceived, and an aesthetically suggestive building raised. The architects' main idea was to put in a complex where students and professionals could relate, learn, and innovate. Legorreta + Legorreta encouraged the clients to make the building ecological, with a fixed maintenance price and considerable savings on energy costs. A good example of this effort is seen in the façades, with their high thermal inertia. The funny spiral shape of the building meets the demands of the site's topology. The entrance is in the center of this spiral, where a large 97-foot-high atrium routes you through the different rooms.

Das Ziel der Technischen Hochschule bestand darin, Studenten und Führungskräfte anzuziehen, die ihre Ausbildung in der Graduiertenschule vervollständigen möchten. Daher wurden innovative Programme entwickelt und ein in ästhetischer Hinsicht äußerst spannendes Gebäude errichtet. Das Hauptanliegen der Architekten war es, eine Anlage zu bauen, in der sich Studenten und Angestellte treffen, lernen und innovativ tätig sein können. Darüber hinaus bewegten Legorreta + Legorreta die Kunden dazu, ein ökologischen Ansprüchen genügendes Gebäude zu bauen, das über ein festes Budget für die Instandhaltung verfügt und beträchtliche Energieeinsparungen ermöglicht. Dieser Aufwand wird beispielhaft an den Fassaden sichtbar, die eine hohe thermische Trägheit besitzen. Die einzigartige Spiralform des Gebäudes gibt die Beschaffenheit des Geländes wieder. Der Zugang befindet sich im Mittelpunkt dieser Spirale, von dessen 9 Meter hohem Atrium-Hof aus die Benutzer in die verschiedenen Bereiche des Gesamtkomplexes gelangen.

L'Institut technologique d'études supérieures avait pour objectif de capter élèves et cadres supérieurs afin qu'ils complètent leur cursus au sein de l'École de commerce. De là des programmes innovants mais également la réalisation d'un bâtiment à l'esthétique séduisante. Les architectes ont eu pour objectif principal la création d'un complexe où les élèves et les professionnels pourraient établir des relations, apprendre et innover. De plus, Legorreta + Legorreta ont suggéré aux clients la construction d'un édifice écologique avec un budget d'entretien fixe et des économies d'énergie considérables. Cet effort est parfaitement symbolisé par les façades dotées d'une inertie thermique élevée. La forme en spirale, si particulière, du bâtiment répond à la configuration du terrain. L'accès se situe au centre de cette spirale où un vaste atrium de 9 mètres de haut distribue les usagers entre les différentes zones du complexe.

L'obiettivo dell'Istituto Tecnològico de Estudios Superiores era quello di accogliere presso la sua struttura un determinato tipo di studenti e di specializzati ad alto livello al fine di completare i loro studi nel settore di programmi innovativi. La Scuola di Specializzazione è nata per questo motivo e venne costruita come un edificio esteticamente attrattivo. Lo scopo principale degli architetti era quello di creare un complesso in cui studentie professionisti potessero relazionarsi, conscere e aggiornarsi. Inoltre Legorreta+Legorreta convinsero i iclienti nel pensare a un edificio "ecologico", ossia con le caratteristiche di un costo di manutenzione fisso e con un risparmio energetico considerevole. Un buon esempio di questo sforzo è reso evidente nelle facciate che hanno una forte inerzia termica. La singolare forma a spirale dell'edificio è in armonia con la morfologia del terreno. L'accesso si trova al centro di questa spirale, dove un grande atrio alto 9 metri divide gli utenti nelle diverse parti del complesso.

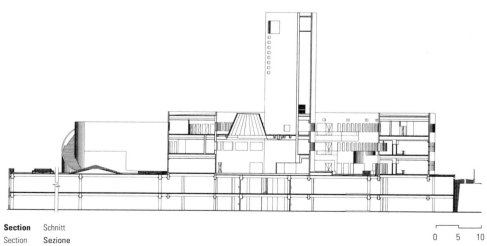

Section   Schnitt
Section   **Sezione**

0   5   10

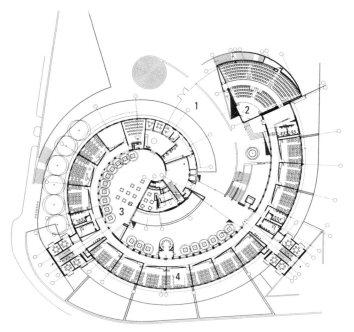

1. **Access**   1. Eingang
2. **Auditorium** 2. Auditorium
3. **Coffee Shop** 3. Cafeteria
4. **Classrooms** 4. Hörsäle

1. Accès   1. Entrata
2. Auditorium   2. Auditorium
3. Cafeteria   3. Caffetteria
4. Salle de classe 4. Aule

Floor of the main building Grundriss des Hauptgebäudes
Étage de premier bâtiment **Pianta dell'edificio principale**

0   5   10

Hotel Sheraton Abandoibarra

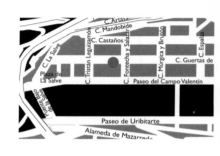

Blv. Víctor María de Lecea & Alameda de Abandoibarra,
Bilbao, Spain

The hotel is part of Ría 2000, the new Bilbao urbanistic development designed to recover the banks of the Nervión River. The building completely occupies the 17,652-square-foot site and is ten stories high plus an attic, set back from the façade line. Taking as a reference point the history and culture of the Basque Lands, the architects drew up plans for a large solid block after the fashion of a sculpture. This was worked according to the program's needs. Windows in the walls bring in sun and the well-lighted complex interior enjoys different interplays of light and shade throughout the day. The rooms range off a large central space eight stories high and the large mullioned windows present views of the city, the mountains, and the river.

Das Hotel ist Teil von Ría 2000, dem neuen Stadtentwicklungskonzept von Bilbao zur Einbeziehung der Ufer des Nervion. Das Gebäude nimmt das Grundstück von 1640 m² vollständig ein und besteht aus 10 Stockwerken und einem etwas hinter die Fassaden zurückgesetzten Penthouse. Der Ausgangspunkt der Architekten waren Geschichte und Kultur des Baskenlandes und sie entwarfen einen massiven Block, den wie eine Skulptur anmutet, die sie nach und nach gemäß der Anforderungen des Funktionskonzeptes bearbeiteten. Die Durchbrüche in den Mauern erlauben den Lichteinfall ins Innere des Komplexes und lassen tagsüber verschiedene Spiele aus Licht und Schatten entstehen. Die Zimmer sind um ein großes, acht Stockmerke hohes Atrium angeordnet. Die nach außen gehenden Fenster, von denen jedes aus neuen quadratischen Öffnungen besteht, ermöglichen Ausblicke auf die Stadt, die Berge und den Fluss.

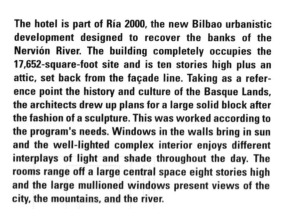

L'hôtel fait partie de Ría 2000, le nouveau projet de développement urbanistique de Bilbao mettant en valeur les rives du Nervión. Le bâtiment occupe la totalité du terrain de 1640 m² et affiche dix étages plus un attique en retrait en regard de la façade. En s'appuyant sur l'histoire et la culture du Pays Basque, les architectes ont projeté un grand bloc massif qu'ils ont taillé au fur et à mesure des besoins du programme, telle une sculpture. Les ouvertures dans les murs laissent le soleil se diffuser à l'intérieur du complexe, créant divers jeux d'ombres et de lumières au cours de la journée. Les chambres s'organisent autour d'un vaste atrium haut de huit étages et jouissent de point de vue sur la ville, les montagnes et la rivière grâce aux fenêtres extérieures, chacune composées de neuf ouvertures carrées.

Il nuovo hotel fa parte del progetto Ría 2000 e regola il nuovo sviluppo urbanistico della città di Bilbao favorendo il recupero delle rive del fiume Nervión. L'edificio occupa completamente il lotto di 1640 m² in cui è collocato e possiede un'altezza di dieci piani piú un attico arretrato rispetto alle facciate. Prendendo quali elementi di referenza la storia e la cultura della nazione Basca, gli architetti hanno progettato un grande blocco massiccio da cui, a mo' di scultura, sono andati scolpendo a seconda delle necessità del programma. La perforazione delle pareti consente la penetrazione del sole all'interno del complesso, creando differenti giochi di luce ed ombra durante l'arco della giornata. Le stanze si dispongono intorno ad un grande atrio di otto piani di altezza e godono della vista della città, delle montagne e del fiume grazie alle finestre che si aprono verso l'esterno, ciascuna delle quali costituita da nove aperture quadrate.

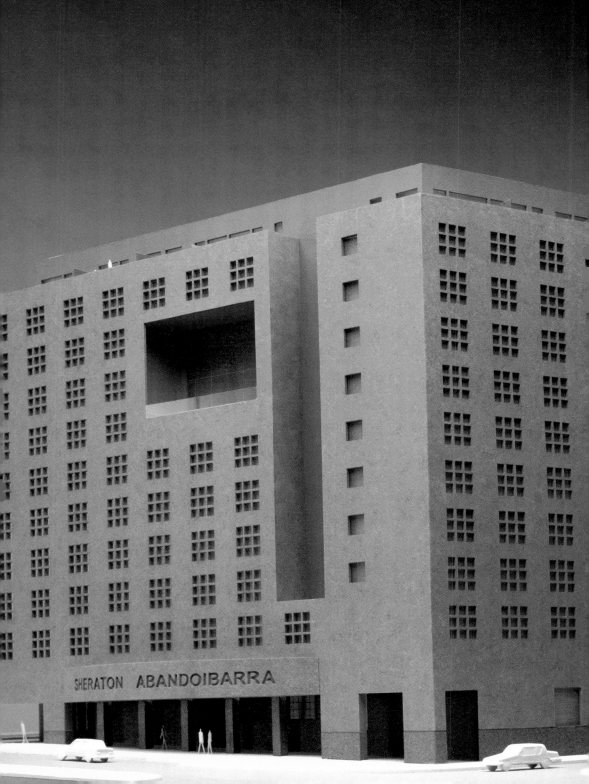

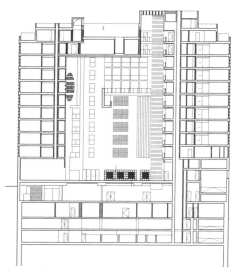

Section Schnitt
Section Sezione

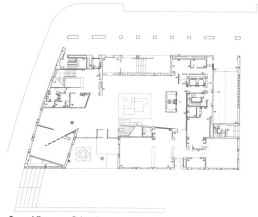

Ground floor Erdgeschoss
Rez-de-chaussée Piano terra

Type floor Geschossgrundriss
Section Type Piano Tipo

0 5 10

V. Lva